Cosplay for Beginners: How to Get Started in Cosplay

Cosplaymom and Kiogenic

ISBN: 1985779811
ISBN-13:9781985779815

DEDICATION

For all the cosplayers, costumers and fans…..including Cosplay
Grandma (pictured on the back cover- as TMNT circa 1986)

CONTENTS

Introduction

1   Choosing Your First Cosplay   1

2   Build or Buy the Costume?   8

3   Resources: What do You Need to Build Your Cosplay?   13

4   Learn How: Get Some Advice and Learn Some Techniques   21

5   Go Shopping for Cosplay Materials   27

6   Making Your Cosplay   35

7   Join the Cosplay Community   39

8   How to Perform Your Cosplay   42

9   Show off Your Cosplay!   45

10   Advice for Attending Cosplay Conventions   48

Conclusion

ACKNOWLEDGMENTS

Many thanks to "Bat Brad" for tech support, Brandon, Darren and Jeff at the Eternal Armory, Flash, and everyone at the Costuming Guild of the Ozarks and Sammy Jo

Introduction: What is Cosplay?

Have you ever seen someone dressed as a Jedi Knight from *Star Wars?* Have you been to *Harry Potter* film in a crowd full of people in Gryffindor robes armed with wands? If you have, then you know what cosplay looks like. What is cosplay? It's a fun, creative and positive way to share your love of a film, television show, video game, book or other media with other people who love the same thing. The term, "cosplay" comes from the Japanese, and has the two important parts of the activity right in the word: "cos" for "costume" and "play" for, well, "play." To cosplay is to wear the costume of a character that you like, from a franchise that you like, and perform, or "play" at being that character. Cosplayers either buy or make their costumes, and then go to conventions or meet-ups where they can make friends and meet other people who like the same things that they do. It's an enjoyable and healthy way to express your creativity, to make life-long friends and learn about new shows and games that you might want to try.

I'm writing this guide in partnership with my daughter, the artist Kiogenic. Kiogenic and I started participating in cosplay in 2013, when one of her art teachers introduced her to the style of art called steampunk. We both loved it, and set out to make whole steampunk costumes. We begged old jewelry from friends and family, scoured thrift shops and learned to solder.

When we were ready, we found a convention nearby that would have other fans of steampunk art. We went, and it's not too much of a stretch to say it changed our lives- we had a wonderful time, made friends, and learned about other types of art and media that we might like to try.

Our first Cosplays! Kiogenic as The Artist- A Steampunk Timelord
and my cosplay of a Steampunk Smuggler- Amelia Elizabeth Hawkhurst Avery

My daughter and I are writing this guide because we love cosplay: we love the cosplay community, the excitement of a convention, the people we meet and the skills we can build in making a cosplay. We want to share this imaginative and exciting hobby with more people and show everyone how much fun they can have. Please read on for tips and hints about how to choose, build, perform and show off your cosplay!

Chapter 1- Choosing Your First Cosplay: How to Get Started

What Do You Like and Who Do You Like?

So you want to get into Cosplay. Great! The first thing you need to do is choose your first character. Who, (or what), do you want to Cosplay? Remember, cosplay is creative. It's open, it's flexible, so you can really choose whoever or whatever you want!

A good place to start is by picking a character from a form of media that you know really well and enjoy watching, reading or playing. To picture yourself cosplaying a specific character, try asking yourself these questions:

- What is my favorite show/movie/game/book?
- Who is my favorite character in that show/movie/game/book?
- Which is the character that I would most like to be like, or the character with whom I identify the most?
- Would it be fun to pretend to be that character?

Let's say that you like the game *Overwatch*. *Overwatch* has lots of different characters, male, female, human, non-human......if you could be any of them, who would you pick? That's a place to start.

Remember that you don't always have to be the good guy. Yes, you can be Luke, or Link, or Princess Peach, but would it be fun to be the bad guy for a day? Ursula from *The Little Mermaid?* Or maybe Voldemort?

Creativity and Original Characters

Here's another approach. As I mentioned, Kiogenic and I started out doing Steampunk, and we invented our own characters. Maybe there is a style or universe or you like that would allow you to create your own costume. Spend some time looking around and see what appeals to you. You can check out Lolita fashion, steampunk style and medieval outfits. Or maybe you like Skyrim or Star Wars? You can be an original character from that universe without having to cosplay a particular figure from the franchise that people might recognize.

I'm a big fan of JRR Tolkien (who wrote the *Lord of the Rings* trilogy). For my second cosplay, I chose to be an elf. I didn't want to be Galadriel or Elrond, I wanted to be an individual and original elf. So I searched through Tolkien's book, the *Simarillion,* and found an elf that I thought fit my personality, Melian of the Valar, lover of trees. And I made my own Melian costume- out of an old prom dress, a suit from the thrift store, some of my grandmother's old jewelry and a pair of ears I bought online.

You can do the same. You can pick a character from a book, a song or a podcast that has no visual reference, per se. So you get to pick what that person looks like! I immediately recognize the cosplayers who are cosplaying Cecil from *Welcome to Night Vale* when I see them at conventions. While the show is a podcast, and none of us know exactly what Cecil looks like, we all know he's a radio broadcaster, and that the podcast's signature color is purple. When I see young men and women dressed as radio broadcasters with touches of purple (and sometimes the podcast's logo) I know exactly who they are.

Put Your Own Spin on a Character

It's also possible and popular to take a character like, for example, Nightwing (a hero from DC comics) and re-design his costume to suit your own personal preference. Maybe you don't like his Arkham get up and the new outfit he wears in DC Rebirth isn't what you're are really looking for in a cosplay.

That's ok! If you like the character, and would like to

cosplay him, you can make your own take on it. This can be anything from a cyber-punk rendition of the character with a futuristic armor, goggles and an LED symbol on his chest (as opposed to a preexisting more traditional design of a skin-tight suit with minimal armor and domino mask). Or you can take the cosplay in a more casual direction and don a custom leather jacket with Nightwing-centric patches and symbol on the back, black jeans and combat boots. Fans of the series will still recognize you as that character and as long as you feel comfortable in the design you chose, that's the most important thing.

The moral here is that cosplay celebrates creativity. Feel free to choose to be Princess Leia or Batman, but also know that you can have fun and be who you want to be by using your imagination and inventing something new!

Cosplay is for Everyone: The Only Rule is to Cosplay What You Love

So if you are a woman, can you cosplay a male character? Yes. If you are human can you cosplay a robot? Yes. If you are full-figured, can you cosplay someone slim? Yes. If you are 70 years old can you cosplay Elsa from *Frozen?* Yes. If you are skinny, can you cosplay a muscular character? Yes.

Cosplay is for everyone, of every gender, shape, ethnicity and religion. We are not going to promise you that you will never get a negative comment about how you "don't look enough like the character." We wish we could, but this can and will happen. The thing is, though, that the vast, overwhelming majority of the cosplay community is open, welcoming and warm.

Remember that, both when you see others in cosplay, and when you step out of your car or your hotel room in your own costume. Be kind. Be enthusiastic. Celebrate yourself and your fellow cosplayers' creativity and ignore those who choose to be mean.

At Kiogenic's and my first convention, I went to a panel run by a professional cosplayer who was so good that people paid him to come to their events. His advice was to welcome everybody, no matter how good or bad, elaborate or simple their costume. He said: "it doesn't matter if a person's costume is just a pair of goggles. If it is, that's GREAT." He was pointing out that we are all there for the fun, to explore and play, and we can all be better community members by just being positive.

If you see someone using her hijab as part of her cosplay, compliment her ingenuity! If you see an older person, dressed as a princess, tell him or her how pretty s/he looks! Be there for each other and for yourself. Give compliments and remember and hold on to the compliments that you receive. Let any negativity go, and all of us will have even more fun.

Chapter 2- Build or Buy the Costume?

So you've selected a character that you'd like to invent, or one you'd like to assume the identity of. Great! The next question that you should ask yourself is: "should I build or buy my costume?" There is no wrong answer to this question!

Do I Need to Build My Own Cosplay?

Do you need to? Probably not. Would you like to? Very possibly! There is no reason you can't buy your cosplay. There are lots of places that you can go to buy what you need for any number of cosplays. Online stores that sell premade costumes or cosplayers that you can commission to make your cosplay specifically tailored to you can be a good place to look. Especially if your costume is a well-known and popular character like a major superhero or comic book figure, you can probably find a ready-made costume that you can put on and be ready to go!

So why would you want to build your own? There are several reasons to consider making your own cosplay:

- <u>It will fit you better.</u>
  Store-bought and ready-made costumes are easy, but they are made to fit as many people as possible, not just you. A costume you buy at the costume store may be too long, too short, too wide or too skinny. A costume bought online is even riskier, since you can't try it on or hold it up to you before you purchase it. One of Kiogenic's friends bought a Ruby (from RWBY) cosplay online and was terribly disappointed in the fit. It's just harder when something isn't made for you.

  If you make your own cosplay, it will be made just for you, and you can adjust and plan to fit your unique shape.

Even if you have commissioned someone to make said costume and they have all your specifications and measurements it still is a possibility that when your costume arrives it may not fit you one hundred percent well.

- <u>You will be more proud of it.</u>
    Again, there is nothing wrong with buying a costume, but you'll have to trust us when we say that investing not just your money, but your time and talent into making your cosplay will give you that much more confidence when you walk the floor of a convention in it. When people say, "I love your cosplay! Where did you get it!?" imagine how good you'll feel if you can say "I MADE it!"

- <u>It's a great conversation starter.</u>

    One of the reasons we all like to go to conventions is that we meet other people with the same interests who can become friends. If you make your costume, you can talk to others easily about techniques and tips. You'll know more to compliment others' work and can swap ideas and stories.

- <u>You can compete in cosplay competitions.</u>

    Many conventions and events will have competitions for cosplayers in different categories, including "novice!" How fun would it be to show off your hard work on stage? While some of these competitions will allow you compete in store-bought costumes, all will still ask you to explain what you, personally, made in your costume, and you'll receive more points for your own work.

We know this won't be possible for everyone, but we'd like to encourage you to make your own costume. Read on for tips on how to make that possible!

Choosing Your Character Wisely: Simple or Complex?

Whether your build or buy, you should look at possible characters with a simple question in mind: is that costume simple or complex? Since there are so many choices, we suggest that you start with a look that will be simpler and less expensive in time and money to achieve.

For example, you may love the television show *Doctor Who*. In thinking about that show, you will probably realize that it's going to be easier to make a Doctor or companion costume (which are specific kinds of clothes with some accessories) than it will be to make a Dalek costume (which is an evil robot.) Buying or building, cosplays built around "street clothes" are going to be both cheaper and easier.

Closet Cosplay

There are lots of cosplays from movies, books and television programs where you can begin with an outfit of "regular" clothes, and add some touches to turn it into a cosplay more cheaply and easily. Some of these things you may even already have at home! There's a name for this kind of cosplay: closet cosplay. Use the things in your (and your family's) closet!

Kiogenic's first closet cosplay was of the anime character Ciel from *Black Butler*. There was an event in town, and she wanted to wear a new cosplay, but we were low on time and even lower on money. So she went "shopping" at home.

Kiogenic as Ciel

For this cosplay, she used things from her closet and around the house. Long socks, cut off leggings (for shorts), a jacket and shirt she already owned and a pair of black shoes. To add the distinctly Ciel touches, she made a tie out of a piece of blue ribbon, an eye patch from some elastic and a piece of cardboard covered in felt, and a cane from an old curtain rod and some ribbons. The one store-bought item was a wig she already had.

When we got to the venue, we hadn't even gotten in the doors when a group of young people yelled "Hi Ciel!!!!!!!!" and asked to take her picture. While this cosplay wasn't fancy, expensive or perfect, it was fun, people recognized it immediately, and she had a great time.

This story illustrates how you can take clothes from your closet and add a few easy, specialized props to make it cosplay. Want to be a Harry Potter wizard? You can wear street clothes and carry a wand. A character from the *Walking Dead* can be you in dirty clothes with a baseball bat or other improvised "weapon" (though please see the tips on checking the rules on props in Chapter 9)

Think about what you can do with what you already have! Your own version of a Time Lord with a homemade sonic screwdriver? Peter Parker as a student/photographer with a camera? One of the kids from *Stranger Things* with Eggos? Choosing a simple costume can be fun and easy!

Chapter 3- Resources: What do You Need to Build your Cosplay?

So you've decided on a character- either a specific character from the franchise canon, or your own original character. That means that it's time to evaluate the resources you will need to make this cosplay happen! First, find a good image to work off of. Then, time, money and skills are the three main things you should consider.

Find Your Reference Photo

Once you've selected your character, it's time to find good reference photos for you to use as a guide in building or putting together your cosplay. Reference photos will be a key tool for you whether you choose to build or buy your cosplay.

The best first step is to do an image search on google, yahoo, or whatever your favorite search engine is (on google, for example, the "image" option is in the upper right hand corner of the main google page, or if you do a search, "images" will appear on the left under the search box in your results). You can click on "image" any time to just get a page of different image choices. As cosplay has become more popular, and people have shown more attention to detail, media creators have increasingly even provided moving images that show a 360-degree view of the character all the way around, so you can see what the back of the costume looks like!

For a specific character like, say, Wonder Woman, there will be lots of choices. You can then choose between a comic-book version, the Lynda Carter Version or the Gal Gadot version of the supersuit, or the street clothes of any of those Wonder Woman choices. This step can help you focus on what is achievable based on your resources.

Maybe you can't swing the superhero suit quite yet- but you can still cosplay Wonder Woman in her secretarial uniform (for the 1970's version) or what she is wearing when she works at Louvre at the beginning and end of the 2017 movie. We recommend that you save and print out copies of the look that you are wanting to achieve, since you'll want to go back to it again and again as you put the cosplay together.

If you are creating an original character, reference photos will still be important. Print out several versions of the "look" that you are going for. If your character will be a steampunk scientist, do an image search for just that "steampunk scientist" and then one more generally for "steampunk." Choose the images that look like you might be able to handle making that outfit, feeling free to mix and match elements of different styles or designs you find in your image search.

How Much Time Can You Spend on Your Costume?

Making a cosplay should be fun. We don't want anyone to lose out on that part of the activity because they were too stressed by the schedule to enjoy it.

My good friend Sarah, another cosplay mom in England, was determined to build a Rocket Raccoon cosplay for her first cosplay. She had the skills and the talent, but burned herself out trying to work full time and get the costume done. She eventually finished the costume, but only after letting it sit for a year and coming back to it.

Sarah as Rocket

It's easy to get excited about something super-elaborate costume idea, but you may end up not being able to get it done in time. Why be disappointed and frustrated your first, or even second time out? For your first cosplay especially, we recommend that you look at your time frame realistically.

There are several things to consider when you're planning the costume. You may choose to go more elaborate or simpler, depending on your answers to these questions:

- Do you have a deadline? For example, are you making this costume for a convention, party, meet-up or other event that has a fixed deadline? If so, that's your schedule, and to have a good experience, you need to be realistic about how much time between then and now that you have.
- How much of each day can you devote to the project? Are you in school? Working? When do you plan on being able

to work on this? If you are in school and working, for example, you'll only have a few hours per day or week that you can devote to putting your cosplay together.

- Do you feel like you have a lot of skills going in, or are you going to have to learn a bunch of stuff to make this costume? Remember that learning will take time too.

Once you've done a true reckoning of the time you have, you can better make choices about how fancy or elaborate you want to go. As you plan out your schedule, remember to allow time for:

- Looking at reference photos
- Shopping for clothes and materials
- Learning any techniques you need
- Actually putting the cosplay together.

Our advice too would be to build in "iterative process" time. My husband, Kiogenic's stepdad (who we call "tech support"), always reminds us that creating things is an "iterative process."

Tech Support is a scientist, and he knows that you will usually arrive at a better product or result if you keep in mind that work often happens by trial and error. Remember that you're a noob. You may be happy with your first attempt to make a wand or sonic screwdriver. But you may be even happier if you let yourself try and then try again, using what you've learned to improve on your prop or costume the next time!

This means though, that if you have the time, you should schedule the time to maybe have to, or want to do something over again.

One last thought- if you have more money than time, always keep in reserve the option to order parts of your cosplay that you don't have time to make. Just keep in mind that many cosplay-specific items like wigs come from China or Japan, and the shipping for things coming internationally can take many weeks.

How Much Money Can You Spend on Your Costume?

Don't worry, making a cosplay can be very inexpensive. Depending on what you can find around the house, you can put together a very respectable cosplay for less than $30. However, just like with time, the key is to be realistic about how much money you have. The first thing to do is give yourself a budget- $30, $50, $100, whatever works for you.

What your financial budget is, similar to what your time budget is, should help you determine exactly how fancy or elaborate you can afford to be for this first cosplay. It can help you even decide between several simple choices.

Let's say you would like to be able to do either Dipper Pines from *Gravity falls* or Bob Belcher from *Bob's Burgers*. We suggest you make a list of all the things that you need for both costumes. For example:

- Dipper
  - Blue and white baseball cap with a pine tree
  - Red t-shirt
  - Navy blue vest
  - Grey shorts
  - Black sneakers
  - Knee high athletic socks
  - Prop journal

- Bob:
  - Jeans
  - White t-shirt
  - gray jeans or pants
  - white apron with pocket
  - mustache
  - prop hamburger

On both of these lists there are things you may already have. Mark, or check those off as "done." Hooray!

Now look at the things you don't have, and price them online or in thrift shops. If you don't have a hat, how much will it cost online? Are there any at your local Walmart? Fill in those prices. What about your props? Can you make a journal or hamburger out of things in your house? Will you have to buy paint or markers? Fill in those prices.

Once you are done, you can compare and see which fits your budget best. This can help you stay on-budget and on-task and pick the cosplay that best suits how much money you have to spend.

What Costuming Skills Do You Already Have?

Ok, you've looked at your budgets for time and money. Now it's time to evaluate your skills- what do you already know that can help you make this costume happen?

Do you know how to sew? To draw? Have you used a hot glue gun before? Maybe you knit? Or maybe your best skill is thrift shopping? Each of these skills can help you decide how you are going to proceed with your cosplay.

If you know how to sew, consider evaluating your closet, or the closet of your family to see if there are things you can repurpose. If you don't have lots of available material, thrift shops sell clothing as cheap as less than a dollar per piece. Consider gathering material from multiple locations to sew the items you need for your cosplay.

If you don't sew, but know your way around a hot glue gun, that can be a great alternative to sewing. This year, Kiogenic made her Halloween outfit while she was away at college in part by hot gluing one cheap black skirt to another, longer cheap black skirt to make a cloak and hood.

If your major talent is drawing or painting, then cardboard can be your best bet. Kiogenic's friend Sam once put together a great Ringo Starr cosplay that was anchored by a large, yellow submarine that she designed and drew on a large piece of cardboard with markers. This was cheap, fun and extremely effective! (Everyone knew exactly who she was, and loved it!)

Sam as Ringo

Finally, as we will discuss later, one of the best skills you can have for cosplay is thrift shop intel. At our house, we like to call Macklemore's song "Thrift Shop" the "Cosplay Anthem." Whether you are making props, costumes or just looking for gray slacks for your Bob's Burgers cosplay, go pop some tags. Thrift shops are your friend.

Bonus Tip: Using a Cosplanner

If you know that you could use some help getting organized, consider checking out cosplanner.com. Cosplanner is a app designed specifically for cosplayers to organize cosplay ideas, budgets, materials and timelines!

Cosplanner will help you store all your reference photos, list all the items you've bought and keep you on budget and provides a calendar to list upcoming events. When you want, when you are done, you can then share your cosplays.

Chapter 4- Learn How to Build your Cosplay: Get Some Advice and Learn Some Techniques

You've picked a character, you have a reference photo, and you've budgeted time and money. What next? It's time to get some advice from people who have been in your shoes before. As we've mentioned, the cosplay community is welcoming and encouraging, and if you are looking for help and advice on how to design, build or create any part of a cosplay, there are lots of sources of information available to you on the internet.

YouTube Videos

You can certainly just google "how to make a Gravity Falls Journal" (or whatever it is you are hoping to make.) Following up on our Dipper idea, however, I just looked up "how to make a gravity falls journal" on YouTube, and under the heading "how to make a gravity falls journal," I got pages and pages of results for making the prop out of just paper and cardboard, a note book, hardcover book and even wood. The videos also have a wide range of how to do the detailing on the cover from layered paper, air dry clay and even metal. This is just an example of how much information is out there, and on YouTube, in easy to follow step-by-step tutorials.

Many cosplayers have their own YouTube channels as well where they have tutorials and/or vlogs of themselves cosplaying characters. Kiogenic has a YouTube channel, for example, under her name, Kiogenic that features videos of she and her friends doing Gorillaz cosplay.

So another tip is to go to YouTube and just search for cosplay tutorials on the thing or the style you'd like to cosplay. If, for example, you are a fan of *Attack on Titan*, there are dozens of walk-throughs, make-up tutorials, and step-by-step videos of how to make specific pieces of the costumes (either of the titans or the warriors). Some are even labelled with how to do the costume cheaply.

This is true for nearly any costume that you might want to build. Check out these videos, they will likely save you time and money and help you get what you are looking for more cheaply.

Online Cosplay and Costuming Communities

In addition to online tutorials on YouTube, there are also many places on the internet that offer general advice, or step-by-step instructions on building things. A search will take you to many of them, but we would like to profile a few.

<u>Fandom Forums</u>

There are many active websites dedicated to specific films, televisions, video games and comics. These usually aren't very hard to find- they will normally show up in the first page of results in a google search for your favorite show.

These websites have forums, which are question and answer pages, where people talk about specific problems and solutions related to building cosplays related to the game, comic or show. You can just read what's already there, or you can ask a question and get some help from people who like the same things you do and are building similar cosplays.

One site that Kiogenic has used and finds very helpful is a good example of this kind of community. The 405th Infantry Division (https://www.405th.com/forums/) is a website for the video game Halo, that caters specifically to the costume and prop-making community.

This site offers particularly helpful information and tools such as pepakura files for armor-making. (Pepakura is a sort of advanced origami paper craft that is printed with numbers that you match up to make the helmet or other piece.)

This is a Halo Mark VI helmet Kiogenic formed using a pepakura file

We encourage you to look for sites related to the things you love, and especially look for the prop and costuming versions of those sites.

Cosplay.com

The website www.cosplay.com, a clearing house and online meet-up for cosplayers from all over the world, has a great series of discussions on making your cosplay, under "Cosplay Construction." When you go to the site, you'll click on the "forums" tab at the top, and then scroll down to find the section with discussions on how to make things. On the site, these are divided into categories such as "sewing/fabric crafts," "wigs and hair," "make-up and eye contacts," and a general "cosplay tutorials."

There is even, on cosplay.com a "marketplace" for both those who have skills to offer in building cosplays (and who take commissions) and also a place for people who want to buy pieces, props, or even full cosplays to look for the best deal and talk to vendors.

That's one real value of this kind of site: the ability to talk, ask questions to other cosplayers. If you join the site (which is free), you can post a question on a thread, or start a whole new thread asking a question. This can help connect you to people who have experience with the materials you are using or what you are trying to make and many of these folks have great ideas that you may not have thought of for easier, or cheaper ways to construct costumes.

When Kiogenic and I first started cosplaying, I started a thread called "cosplay parenting" to talk to other parents of cosplayers (and cosplay parents) about any number of things, from budgeting to safety at conventions. I learned a lot and made friends around the world that I still have today!

Use Your Friend and Family Resources

Do you have handy folks in the family? Does grandma or grandpa sew? Do you have an uncle or aunt with a garage full of tools? Maybe you have a friend who is a welder? It's time to make use of these family connections!

When we started cosplaying, my dad (Kiogenic's grandfather) taught us to solder, and let us use his soldering iron. He took us to his workshop and even sent us home with an armful of supplies and materials. Once my aunts found out we were making steampunk jewelry, they sent us all their old jewelry, and my grandfather's jewelry-making tools that had been sitting in an attic. Kiogenic's uncle, the welder, bent some metal for us later.

The next time you're with your friends and family, get them to talk about what they like to do, or what they can do, and see if they are willing to share some expertise. Older folks especially, neighbors, grandparents, etc., would often love you to come visit more often, and would really enjoy the chance to help you with stuff. It can be a very rewarding experience and do a lot for people's self-esteem to be the "expert" who is helping you, so don't be shy to ask. You may even discover that they have skills or interests that you didn't even know about!

Just this week, I had an email from one of my students (I teach college), saying that she had heard through the grapevine that Kiogenic and I might be able to help her with a cosplay. I told her that Kiogenic was at school, but that I would be happy to help. She came over with two turtlenecks and I helped her figure out how to sew them together to make a Star Trek command jersey.

YouTube Channels

As mentioned, like all kinds of interests on YouTube, There are specific channels dedicated to sharing information on cosplay. Make up is one example. There are many, many YouTube Channels devoted to make-up. This can range from channels about special effects makeup like Glam&Gore who combines all different kinds of beauty, and SFX make-up as well. There are other make-up centric videos as well that are good for those unfamiliar with beauty make-up and want to incorporate that element onto their cosplay.

There are also channels like Evil Ted Smith who create a huge variety of armor and props with only EVA foam. He covers everything from basic tools you will need and how to make a pattern for armor, to how to build form fitting chest plates and finishing a piece with shading and aging.

Kiogenic learned most of what she knows about cosplay

makeup, prop and armor construction and wig styling from channels like these as well as individual YouTube videos she still will refer back to. Other resources are also extremely helpful but for visual-learners tutorial videos are your most valuable resource.

Ask, Ask, Ask at Stores

It's been a long time since I worked retail (and I did so only briefly.) But I remember how boring it can be. Therefore, I understand that when people ask Kiogenic and I "what is this for" they may really be interested in knowing!

It is a lot more fun and more interesting to talk to someone seeking "how to advice" than just to get complained at or ignored. So my advice is to ask the folks at the stores if they have advice or guidance. Many a time we have been in a hardware or craft store buying cosplay materials, and we've run into employees who are delighted to talk about what we are making, and offer their advice or tips.

(As a note, however? Older folks especially, but even younger ones won't necessarily know what "cosplay" is. However, you can totally get your point across with "I'm making a costume" or "I'm making a prop for a costume.")

Chapter 5- Go Shopping for Cosplay Materials

After you've decided on a cosplay and spent some time looking at the advice and tutorials about what other people have done, you'll have a good idea of the things you need to buy to build your first cosplay. Depending on what you will be doing or trying to make, you'll need a variety of different materials and tools. In this chapter, we're going to recommend and go over the basics that are most likely to apply to everyone.

Thrift Shopping for Cosplay

As we mentioned above, the ability to engage in savvy thrift shopping is a key tool in any cosplayer's repertoire. When Kiogenic went to college in a different city, one of the first places she found and marked as a key landmark was the closest Goodwill store.

It might sound simple- "go to thrift shop," but there are actually some ins and outs that we can recommend to you when it comes to thrift shopping in your area. This is cosplay shopping advice, built from years of experience.

- Not all thrift shops are equal or identical
  When you are getting started, be sure to visit all the shops that are convenient to you. You will find that the kinds of things, the variety of things, the quantity of things and the quality of things will vary from shop to shop. For example, in our hometown, we know one particular thrift shop almost always has the best selection and prices on clothing. Another shop, however, has a better and more complete selection of housewares and hardwares that we might need for props. Check out all your options, and

learn where you'll have the best chance of finding the pieces you need.

- Don't judge a book by its cover (or a shop by its curb appeal.)
Some thrift shops, ok, *many* thrift shops look like dumps from the outside. This is not a problem! What money they are not spending on the layout or look of the store often comes back to you in lower prices. Items may be dirtier or less shiny, but you can (and should) wash the clothes, and almost everything else cleans right up! Look for the dumpy stores. The biggest and fanciest stores are also often the most picked-over, with the least selection of items.

- Size isn't everything
Also keep in mind that the store, like a TARDIS, may actually be bigger on the inside. One of our favorite thrift shops in our hometown only looks like a small storefront from the street, but once you are inside, it goes all the way back into the building and is actually very big. (It's the one with the best hardware and house wares.- The gauntlet I'm wearing in that first steampunk cosplay is part of a candleholder I bought there.)

- Learn the sales rotations.
Many major stores (like Goodwill, the DAV or the Salvation Army) have sales on their already super-cheap items. Many times again, these sales come in regular rotations. For example, does your local Goodwill do half off clothes every Thursday? Does the DAV always have holiday sales? Knowing this stuff can help you save even more money.

- <u>If you are looking for something specific, ASK.</u>
  Just yesterday, in the middle of writing this project, Kiogenic and I were out thrift shopping, looking for an extra sewing machine for her to take back to college with her. We went into one of those "bigger on the inside" thrift shops where I had spotted a potential machine a few days before. The one we were looking for was already gone, but when I mentioned this to an employee, she showed us not one, but TWO of the precious all-metal ones that were hiding in cabinets! Huge score!

Basic Costuming Tools and Supplies

Whatever cosplay you choose to make will obviously require certain specific tools and supplies. Since we don't know what you are thinking, we can't make a perfect list that will fill all your needs. What we can do is give you a list of commonly used supplies and tools that will work for a wide variety of costumes, both your first, and subsequent costumes!

Many of the things on this list don't have to be new or fancy/expensive. Check your local craft and fabric stores (Hobby Lobby/JoAnn/Michaels) for coupons and sales. You can check thrift stores and discount stores. You can also often thrift or garage sale shop these things, and you may have some of them around the house!

You can use this list as a starting point to build a tool chest of cosplay equipment. This list will keep you ready to go for quite a while.

Tools

- A tool-chest or sturdy box

Now, if you want to, or have access to an actual tool-box, that's great. But it's really not necessary. What you will need is one place to keep all your materials, tools, and pieces of your costume in progress. This can be a sturdy cardboard box, a small chest or a milk crate. This is important so you don't have to chase around all your stuff when you are ready to work, and it will help you to transport your costume and emergency supplies when you go out to a convention or meet up.

- Scissor(s)

  If your budget allows it, we would recommend 2 pair of scissors. Why? Because often you're going to want to cut wire, or plastic or something tough that will mess up the edge on your good scissors. Your scissors can be cheap as long as you mark, and keep separate the ones you use for fabric (those are the good ones) and the "utility" scissors that you're going to use for everything from duct tape to craft foam. A fine edge is really essential for cutting fabric. Guard your fabric scissors!

- Hot Glue Gun(s)

  Glue, and hot glue, are cosplayers' friends, especially if you don't have access to a sewing machine or know how to sew. Hot glue guns come in two varieties- high heat and low heat. You need a different gun for each option. So once again, if your budget will allow it, get both.

  Consider what you will be putting together. A high-temp glue gun is best when you need a quick and strong bond. High-temp works best on tougher and more durable materials like cardboard, leather, wood, metal and plastics. This is the gun you will need for most props. A low-temp glue gun is better for more delicate materials that can't take as much heat. You would use this on silky fabrics, paper, craft foam and ribbon.

Note: Hot glue and hot glue guns are not for the weak or the careless! One of Kiogenic's university professors recently told her "they ruin everything they touch." That's not entirely true, but it's not a bad caution. As useful as they are, using a hot glue gun can burn you and burn you badly (in addition to ruining delicate materials). Especially with a high-temp gun, the glue that comes out is like napalm- ridiculously hot and STICKY. Please be careful. Kiogenic has far too many bad burn scars from getting hot glue on her skin.

- Needle and thread
  This is a key (and very cheap) item that is a must for small work and finishing. You can buy a needle and a spool of thread for very little money, and they can save your cosplay. This is also a better option for things like buttons and other small decorative pieces that don't work with glue.

- Seam Ripper
  A seam-ripper is a small hook-shaped tool that you buy at a craft or fabric store. You use a seam ripper to take apart clothing at the seams. This is important, because as we noted above, sometimes you will be buying thrift shop clothing to use as basic materials. You'll want to take the clothes apart as cleanly as possible with the fewest rips.

- Fabric paint and brushes/sponges.
  There are a lot of cosplays that you can customize by custom-painting a shirt. You can easily turn a $1 thrift shop t-shirt into a cosplay shirt by painting a Superman logo or arc reactor on it. You can do this by hand, with brushes, or by using a stencil made of a random piece of cardboard. There are lots of stencil patterns online if you do an image search for what you are looking for.

A Note on Sewing Machines

We want to be clear that you don't HAVE to have a sewing machine or know how to use it to get started in cosplay. Hot glue and E-6000 will take you a long way. If you can sew, however, or if you have someone who is willing to teach you a few basic things, a sewing machine is an amazing tool for cosplay, but again, an optional one!

A sewing machine can allow you to make things you can't find, but perhaps even more importantly, it can help you trim and tailor your thrift-shop pieces to fit you better or to create new looks. Home from college for the holidays, Kiogenic went thrift shopping with a vision for a jacket, bought two jackets for three dollars each, and is taking them apart (seam ripper) to sew them back together in a new configuration.

So- if you either have the know-how, or access to someone with some skills, you might want to consider getting a sewing machine. And again, thrift shops are going to be your friend. You can find very reasonably priced machines at thrift shops. We recommend that you just ask as you go around if anyone has any machines.

If they do, as another note, the old-school, all-metal machines can be the best bet for sewing cosplay things. When you are making a cosplay, you often want to sew things that are, well, non-standard. You may be sewing vinyl or nylon belts. You may want to attach something to leather. You may actually want to sew plastic. This is hard on modern-day machines.

When Kiogenic and I first started cosplaying, I had a machine in the house that I used sometimes for simple things like hemming or making curtains. It was older, but still very functional until we started working on cosplay. Then we killed it pretty quickly. Like, non-fixable killed it.

I budgeted money for a new machine, and we picked the new "Singer Heavy-Duty." It lasted about a year and a half. I took it into our local sewing machine shop and the guy asked, "what are you SEWING with this?" I explained, and he gave us some great advice: he said that what we needed was an old-fashioned, all-metal machine from a thrift shop. It's true of sewing machines like everything else: they don't make 'em like they used to. Even though we had picked the machine that was called "heavy-duty," Shawn, our fix-it guy, said that didn't mean much. We needed an old, all-metal model.

So consider that if you are looking for a machine. The great thing is that you might have relative who has one lying around they want to get rid of. My daughter-in-law had just passed one up! Or you might go to a shop and find one for really cheap! We bought two, yesterday, one for $20 and one for $30. And as I was paying, another lady in the store asked if I wanted another!

Whether you are buying a newer or older machine online or at a thrift store, make sure they run before you buy them. Also, the accessories (like a button-holer, bobbins, etc.) are worth more.

Materials

- Craft Foam
  This is a perfect armor material for those new to cosplay. It is extremely accessible and affordable. You can find sheets of varying thickness at Hobby Lobby and even Walmart for less than a dollar a sheet. This is an extremely popular material for cosplay armor and you can find many resources online on how to get started using the material. You only need a good pair of scissors, X-acto knife or utility knife to cut it (depending on thickness).

- Glue Sticks for your Glue Gun

These are relatively inexpensive. Be sure to check that you are buying the right kind for the glue gun you have- there are different sizes (like different sizes of gun) and there are also different sticks for high-temp and low-temp

• E-6000

E-6000 is a glue that is a cosplayer's best friend. It is nearly as effective and adhesive as hot glue, but it's much safer, since it won't burn you. E-6000 holds not quite as well as high-temp hot glue, but nearly as well. It also dries clear (unlike hot glue) so it can be a good choice for finishing work. E-6000 can be bought in big tubes or little. A lot of cosplayers like the smaller tubes because E-6000 has a tendency to dry out in the tube after you've used it once or twice. That's frustrating. However, if you buy the smaller tubes, you're more likely to use it up before it dries out. The drawback to E-6000 is that it is significantly more expensive than hot glue, so you can let your budget be your guide

Chapter 6- Making Your Cosplay

Carve out some space

You are soon going to find out that making your cosplay takes up a lot of space. You'll need both work space and storage space as you go along, so think ahead to where you can put all your stuff. Your housemates or roommates will thank you if you don't leave your cosplay detritus all over.

In the case of Kiogenic and I, we started with a chest. It was a small, wooden box, the kind you can find at IKEA or a thrift shop. We called it the "steampunk chest." It became the big box where all the steampunk pieces and tools went when we tidied up for the night.

We were living on our own in a small apartment, and this was the best bet at that time. We would get out our work in progress, the materials and tools we needed, and spread out over the kitchen table or the living room floor. Then later, we would put the stuff all back in the chest.

You may be a person who doesn't mind the project taking over your living space and having bits strewn about. I'm not here to chide you for being messy. The reality is, however, if you leave stuff out, it runs the risk of getting broken or dirty or messed up. We were once careless with a skirt, and didn't get it put away, and it got something spilled on it.

That can be the issue with workspaces like the kitchen table or living room floor. (If you have pets, the floor is particularly problematic in terms of claws and teeth, but also fur. Cosplay pets are well known for needing to sit on, chew, or run off with your stuff.)

So when Kiogenic and I moved into a house, we dedicated the third bedroom (what for some people is the "guest room" and turned it into the arts and crafts room. This gave us a place to leave the sewing machine permanently out, pieces and tools on easy-to-access shelves and patterns and reference photos tacked up to the wall. It's always a horrendous mess, but I can close the door when company comes or if I need to pretend the mess doesn't exist.

My hairdresser John, who has always been an artist said his Mom did something similar for him when he was young, giving him part of the basement for an art studio.

This may not be an option for you. Not everyone has space available. But I mention it so that you can think in terms of giving yourself some creative space, and making one place for your costuming stuff so you are limiting the chaos for your roommates or family. Is there garage space? Basement space? Could you repurpose a corner of your room?

Lastly, do you have a friend with whom you could share space? Having a co-habitating maker space where you all share tools, materials, etc. can be a great thing to save money and help each other.

Remember That It's An Iterative Process

I mentioned before the necessity of giving yourself a break, and realizing that your first try at something isn't always going to be perfect. In fact, you may not be happy with the first try at all.

This is especially true if you are using materials or techniques that you are trying for the first time. If you can afford it, it can be a really good idea to buy enough materials for a "test run" on whatever you're making. If you want to paint a t-shirt, for example, get an extra one (that doesn't even have to be the right color) and use your stencil on it first. This will help you see what to do and what not to do on the shirt you bought for the final product.

Remember also, that this will all take time. Giving yourself time to be careful, do test runs and do-overs will help reduce your stress as the day of the meet-up, convention or other event approaches.

And again, be patient with yourself. Remember that you are new at this, you are learning, and so are a lot of people around you! Don't be afraid to wear pieces of a cosplay that you don't feel are perfect. Kiogenic is the biggest perfectionist, and I have to remind her that much of what she sees as major flaws- *no one else will notice.* And even if they do, who cares? This is your costume. Do your best and just keep reminding yourself how much you are learning!

What to Do If It All Goes Wrong

Ok, so you've decided to make something, and in the end it all went wrong. You wanted to paint a t-shirt, and spilled non-washable paint on it. Maybe you tried to make a pair of Castiel wings and one side won't stay hot glued together. No worries! This is still a viable cosplay, if you remember a key cosplay rule:

"You can make a ZOMBIE version of anything!"

This is a great rule, because cosplay and cosplayers appreciate creativity and whimsy. As we said before, you can do mash-ups, and make steampunk Joker or mecha Princess Leia. In the same way, you can make zombie Joker or zombie princess Leia.

This is very liberating, because the zombie aesthetic is torn up, chewed-up, bloody and decayed. So it's the perfect way to repurpose a cosplay that went wrong. If one of Castiel's wings is missing, highlight the broken part, add some blood and a vacant stare and you are now ZOMBIE CASTIEL. The same with the t-shirt idea. If the paining went badly, rip it, cover it with blood and now you are "dead" Superman or "zombie" Tony Stark.

Play it up, don't hide it! Have your backstory ready about what happened to your character- (zombie attack? nuclear apocalypse? viral outbreak?) and then lurch and moan when it comes time to hit the convention floor.

This is, by the way, a great way to recycle and reuse old costumes and clothing. You can tear them up and blood smear them to be zombie anything. When I was in Mexico City this year for Mexico City's comicon, I had the good fortune to be there for Day of the Dead. I saw a LOT of zombie *quinceañeras*. (A *quinceañera* is a girl on her 15th birthday party. She traditionally gets a very elaborate prom-style dress that she will only wear once.)

I thought it was brilliant to repurpose the dress for Day of the Dead and the Comicon! I think you can totally do a similar thing with prom dresses and bridesmaid dresses: "Zombie bridesmaids" would be an AMAZING group cosplay!

Chapter 7- Join the Cosplay Community

One of the main reasons that people start participating in cosplay is because it's a great way to meet people, make friends, learn about new movies, shows and games and find people who like the same things you do.

For artistic and introverted folks, it can be hard to get out there and make new friends and meet people. The good news is that the cosplay community is made up of many of those same people! It is totally worth it to put yourself out there to say hi to someone wearing a t-shirt from the same fandom, or who is wearing a costume from the same franchise as yours.

"I really like your cosplay" is a no-fail way to start a conversation with someone. If you've made your own, you can then follow up with, "how did you make your……" or even "where did you get your……"

After talking costumes, you can talk characters or plot lines, and appreciate and enjoy getting excited about the same media that your new friend likes too. The cosplay community is very welcoming, in general, and extremely excited about what they are excited about. And that's a good thing!

So we encourage you to stretch a little- either before, during or after making or buying your costume, join the community and see what's out there! Below are some easy ways to start meeting people, getting advice and making friends. (We'll talk about attending conventions later.)

Online Cosplay Communities

There are lots and LOTS of ways to connect with the cosplay

community online. The only real question is where would you like to try first? There are communities dedicated to particular genres, to particular shows, films and games and communities that identify themselves by age, ethnicity or religion.

If you are on Facebook, that is a great place to start. I personally belong to and follow five Facebook groups that are cosplay-related. One is called "Cosplayers of a Certain Age." This group is for the older-than-40 set who would like the advice and friendship of other older cosplayers. On that page, we offer advice and encouragement, show off our new costumes and talk about future plans.

I also belong to "Cosplay Tutorial Hangout," "Sewing for Steampunk and Cosplay" and "The Costuming Guild of the Ozarks." These are groups that are my go-to for when I need advice on how to make something. People in these groups post questions like: "Does anyone know where I can get a cheap heat gun?" or "what's your advice on making this cape?" Recently, in "Sewing for Steampunk and Cosplay" there was a whole discussion on how to make the hat that Diana Prince wears at the beginning of *Wonder Woman*.

I also belong to a page called "CSM: Cosplay Support Movement." This is a page for folks who are shy, or who may have had a bad experience to come and get encouragement and validation. CSM exists to support everyone's right to cosplay anyone they want. I find it a lovely and positive place.

Finally, I follow our local cosplay club: Springfield Cosplay Group. This is how I find out about events and meet-ups, plans for conventions and other items of note.

My advice would be to just go to Facebook and search "Cosplay" in the "groups" area. You will find literally hundreds of different groups you might like to join and follow. There are groups for specific fandoms (like Star Wars, Anime or Star Trek), tutorial hangouts, cosplay groups for people of color, for gay folks, for plus-size people, pretty much anything you could be asking for.

Cosplay Clubs

Our town isn't very big, but has a cosplay club. It's very possible that yours, or a city near you does as well! Clubs can be a great place to make friends IRL, swap stories or just find some friends to attend events with.

Clubs often plan to attend conventions together, organize meet-ups and picnics, share tools and materials and participate in parades or local festivals. The club I belong to, Springfield Cosplay Group, regularly marches in the local Christmas parade and hosts a cosplay competition at our Japanese Fall Festival. We have a shared fabric vault, and have regular meet-ups with activities and photo shoots.

Cosplay Meet-ups

Once you get involved in online or in-person cosplay community, sometimes you'll find that there are a bunch of you who live close by who could get together just to meet and talk, and do things like take pictures.

This can happen within a general cosplay group, and the meet-up might be of people in cosplays from a whole range of franchises, or you might find a group who are all cosplaying characters from the same fandom.

Our hometown cosplay club organizes several meet-ups, usually four a year. We have met in parks and in library meeting rooms. At a meet-up you'll usually find lots of opportunities for photo shoots, sometimes there's food, and you can make a lot of great friends!

Chapter 8- How to Perform Your Cosplay

You've made, or bought, your cosplay, and now you're ready to perform! It's not just about the outfit, it's about you "playing" the role of that favorite character from a beloved franchise. Remember that cosplay is a compound word, with the "cos" for costume" and the "play" for, well, "play." As the word indicates, this is not only a key part of the practice, but it's designed to be fun! This part of the activity lets you play at being something or someone different for a while, someone braver, or meaner, or nicer, or whatever. It's a chance to experiment with different identities and try on different personas.

The "play" part of cosplay is just as important as the costume. So here are some of our tips on working on that part of your cos-"play."

Know Your Character

- Personality

Now you've probably selected your character because you know and like them. So you should start by making a list of those characteristics or attributes that you really like. Is it strength? Confidence? Beauty? Poise? Grace? Funniness? Think about it and make a list or write some notes.

Not sure what you are wanting or needing to portray? We suggest you do some research. As an example, many characters from movies, television shows or video games have profiles and backstories that you can find on the internet.

Let's say that you want to cosplay Princess Bubblegum from *Adventure Time,* but are sort of stumped on how to "act" like her. The *Adventure Time* wiki is a good place to start. Most popular series have Wikis. Wikis are kind of (but not exactly) like Wikipedia. They are similar in that they are sources of information that allow collaborative editing by users. In the case of the wikis related to shows, games, etc., these are pages of information made and edited by the fans- people like you.

Wikis give detailed information on characters that you might not have noticed, and they do it from the collective base of knowledge about the character and the show. Going back to Princess Bubblegum, if you go to the description of her on the Wiki, you'll find best guess as to age, her origin story, a list of her strengths and abilities (including combat skills) and a whole section on her personality. Finally, in many wikis, and in the one dedicated to Princess Bubblegum, you'll find a list of outfits that she wears, with details on color. This can be very useful to cosplayers!

So if you've found, for example, that your character, Princess Bubblegum, is a scientist and teenager who loves her subjects and parties, think how you'll communicate that in your cosplay!

- Mannerisms

After personality and character, the next thing to do is think about the mannerisms or actions that represent and define your character. Maybe your character always strokes his/her chin or flips his/her hair. Maybe they have a signature line that they always say.

These mannerisms will help you feel like the character, and make it even more obvious who you are cosplaying. When Kiogenic's best friend Sam decided to do some closet cosplay of Benedict Cumberbatch's Sherlock character, all she needed was a long coat and scarf, and the mannerism of folding her hands together in front of her lips. We went out, and people immediately recognized her. Conversely, a friend of mine did Velma (from *Scooby Doo*) one year, and it was her saying "Jinkies!" as much as the orange sweater that sold the cosplay.

So think about your character. Are they confident? Then stand tall. Are they shy? Slouch down and hide your face. Do they always make jokes? Then have a few ready! All these actions and mannerisms will help you communicate and perform your character most successfully, so you are happy in the costume and others will enjoy seeing you in it!

• Practice Posing in Your Costume

This is an important step for two reasons: firstly, you need to be ready when people want to take your photo- (and they WILL want to take your photo!) and you also need to learn how to walk, sit and move in your cosplay.

One of the most fun things about a convention is to have your picture taken, and to take others' photos. When this happens, you want to portray the character you are cosplaying in the moment, in a pose. So once your cosplay is done, spend some time in front of a mirror practicing some poses that are associated with the character. See which one you think looks most like the elements of the character that you are wanting to portray, and be ready to hit that pose in the moment at the event you are attending!

This practice will also give you some experience moving in your costume. It's a chance to check that you can, in fact, raise your hands over your head, walk or sit down. (And if you can't you are forewarned and have a chance to modify the outfit.) Finally- and this isn't for photos- remember that you'll likely want to be able to go to the bathroom in your cosplay.

Chapter 9: Show Off Your Cosplay!

Making YouTube Videos

Going to conventions and meet-ups is a great way to show off your cosplay. You can also, however, make fun videos to share with others who like the same things you do!

This can be easy as using your phone. If you have a smart phone, you can take a video, save it and should be able to upload it directly to YouTube by clicking on the YouTube icon. You can also buy a small handheld camera for less than $50 and use the SD card to upload videos to a computer. Remember that videos take up a lot of storage space, so you'll want to make sure you have enough on whatever device you use. You can ask a friend, a family member, or even better, a fellow cosplayer to take the video.

Think about your setting or backdrop. You'll want to offer some kind of action for a video, so think about where your character might normally go, or what they might normally do, and then think about handy places that might be good sets for your video.

For Kiogenic, we did videos and photo shoots of her Tris (from *Divergent*) cosplay in a parking garage. Parking garages are good for urban or post-apocalyptic settings. For her Gorillaz videos, they used a hotel room at the convention.

There are good online resources on tips for making a cosplay video. There is even (on YouTube!) a nice young cosplayer at a convention giving a how-to lesson on cosplay videos.

Your first video doesn't have to be long or elaborate. It can be you, dressed as Link, from Zelda, frolicking in the park. But it will give you a way to share your cosplay with others. Just beware though, that especially online, people can be unfortunately mean. Don't let any negative comments get you down!

Cosplay Photography

If you're not quite ready for videos, then think about taking good photos of your cosplay. You'll want to share photos on social media (Facebook, Instagram, etc.) so one of the best things you can do is either learn to take great selfies, or work with your friends to take good photos of cosplay. There are lots of tips on sites like cosplay.com, but here are a few ideas.

Keep your background simple

The focus of your photo is your costume. So it's best not to distract from the photo with a cluttered or elaborate background. Choose plain walls, or even learn to take the background out of focus to keep the attention on your great pose and cosplay!

Remember the context of your character

Keep your background simple, yes, but also keep context in mind. If you are Spiderman, staying near a wall is good. If you are Belle, posing in front of a shelf of books is a good idea.

Watch the Light and Beware Your Camera's Built-In Flash

To look best, you'll want a place with good natural light, and few shadows. The more light there is in the space, the more natural your cosplay will look. It's almost never a good idea to use the camera's built-in flash, it washes out the foreground of your costume and make-up!

Check Out What Others Have Done

Go ahead and search for other cosplayers and cosplays in an image search on the internet. See where and how they have posed, and get ideas from that!

If It's in Your Budget- Consider Hiring Someone

There really is a difference in professionally taken photographs and amateur ones. A professional will know all about all of the above, and be able to edit your photos after. Craigslist is a good place to start looking for reasonably priced cosplay photographers.

Chapter 10- Advice for Attending Cosplay Conventions

Conventions- fantasy, science fiction, gaming, anime or a general Comic-con, all are great places to go see others' cosplay and show off your own. Any convention, in any genre will have many folks wandering around in cosplay, and you will fit right in!

There are also many conventions devoted specifically to cosplay. Kiogenic's favorite convention is one held near where we live in Missouri- it's called Cosplacon, and is devoted to all manner of all kinds of cosplay!

Whether you are outgoing or shy, we really recommend that you look around, do an internet search and find some conventions near you! Here are some hints and tips about attending a convention.

Check the Rules

In order to maintain a safe and welcoming place for everyone who attends, conventions have rules governing behavior, and cosplay. It's important to check out these rules in advance. You'll always be able to find them on a convention's website.

Rules usually fall into these categories:

- Badge/registration
  These will be the rules about what areas are only available to people who have registered and who have a badge. Some conventions will let you wander common areas without registering, but you need a badge to go in the vendor/artist's room or any panels and events. Others will require you to register no matter where you are at the convention.

- Harassment/Behavior

  We really like conventions with clear anti-harassment and general behavior policies. These policies usually cover things like "cosplay is not consent"- (which means you can't touch cosplayers without permission- just don't touch anyone without permission, ok?), no means no, stop means stop and "go away" means "go away." These policies mean that if you have a problem you can find a convention volunteer and they will help you.

- Costumes

  This is usually a rule about how little is too little- a rule about nudity. Most conventions will say that "anything smaller than a swimsuit" is too small, but be sure to read the rule to make extra sure your costume is ok.

- Props and "weapons"

  This is also particularly important for cosplayers. We live in sad and dangerous times, and we all want to know that your Punisher weapon isn't real. Therefore, each convention will have rules about prop weapons. Sometimes a convention will require an orange tip on prop guns. Many conventions require you to have your weapon "peace bonded," which means going to a special table/check in stop where a security team will check out your prop and give it a special tag marking it as non-lethal.

  (It goes without saying that you never, ever, use real weapons as props, right?)

Check Out the Schedule

Conventions normally have panels, special presentations, dances, meet-ups and signings. Our advice is to look at the schedule and do a preliminary plan of the time you spend. Many conventions will post their schedules online, so you can look in advance and choose the day you'd like to go, (especially if the price of a whole weekend pass is out of your budget.)

Here's the scoop on different kinds of events that are of specific interest to cosplayers:

- Panels

    Most convention will have a schedule of panels, or workshops, that are run by both fans and experts in their field. These panels often include many of the topics we've talked about here: cosplay construction, photography, etc.

    However, even if you don't find panels specifically related to cosplay, we really encourage you to attend panels related to the fandom of your cosplay (so if you are a Harry Potter cosplayer, go to a Harry Potter panel!) You will meet other fans of the same thing you like, have fun and make friends!

- Tea Parties

    Some conventions will have tea parties organized by members of a specific club or fandom. You usually need to sign up for this kind of event in advance, but it is super-fun. At the tea party, people will be dressed to fit in with the theme, drinks and snacks will be served, and cosplayers and club members will share information about the movie, anime or fandom that they participate in.

- Vendor's Room and Artist's Alley

    Every convention is a primo place to do some shopping! Most conventions divide the items for sale into "vendors," who generally sell manufactured merchandise like t-shirts, figurines or comic books, and "artists" who make their own items to sell. Both are fun to look at (even if you don't have money to spend), but this is also a great place to shop! If you can, bring some spending money!

- Special Events

    Many times, conventions have special events that will be listed in the program. Depending on the kind of convention, this could be a signing with a famous actor, artist or illustrator, a dance or rave, a lecture by an industry member, etc. Sometimes these events will have an extra charge, and sometimes they are free. Sometimes you will need to register for these events, and sometimes you will just stand in a really, really long line. It's a good idea to check the convention schedule to plan ahead for any of these events that you are really interested in!

    And look, especially, for the cosplay competition!

Entering Cosplay Competitions

One very common event at conventions is a cosplay competition. This can be called a contest, a masquerade or a royale, and there may even be more than one. Whether you want to just watch the competition to see everyone's amazing cosplays, or if you think you'd like to compete, check out the cosplay competition!

Competitions can be a fun and rewarding way to show off your hard work in putting together a costume, and have an opportunity to go on stage and have fun! Competitions are generally divided into categories, so don't worry, you will likely have the opportunity to compete against other "beginners" and not the "experts" with elaborate armor and weapons.

At Kiogenic's and my first convention, we entered as "beginners" and we both won an award. Kiogenic won a special "judge's choice" and I won an honorable mention. It made both of us feel great!

But at other conventions, Kiogenic has entered and not won. And that's ok too! We don't want you to think that the only reason to enter is because you have to win. Entering a cosplay competition is about more than just winning. You'll meet other cosplayers, have a chance to explain your work, get great feedback and have fun!

A cosplay competition usually comes in two parts, so be sure to be ready for both. First, there will be pre-judging. Pre-judging is when you either stand in line, or get a time to go, on your own, in front of the judges. You will show them your reference photo, explain your costume (who you are, etc.) and also have a chance to explain which parts of the costume you made.

The second part will be the stage presentation. This is the part that happens in front of a (usually) very large audience. It is often the biggest event of a competition. You'll go on stage and perform your cosplay. You can read lines, do a dance, pose, or whatever you find appropriate!

Then you will wait for the results!

If you think you'd like to enter, here are some tips for entering a cosplay contest.

- Have your reference photos ready and easy to get access. Judges aren't always going to be familiar with the character you are cosplaying, or the universe you are cosplaying from. Be ready to show them an image that communicates what you were going for in your costume. They will have lots of cosplayers to judge, and limited time, and they will appreciate you having your reference photo ready.

- <u>Plan and practice your stage "act"</u>
  Many cosplay competitions are judged on both your costume and how well you "play" it. Be ready to do something besides stand still on the stage.

- <u>Be ready to spend a lot of time</u>
  While Kiogenic and I still cosplay, we don't enter as many competitions, because they will typically take your whole day. The whole process takes quite a bit of time, and there is lots of standing around. If you choose to enter, just be ready for that to be your activity for most of the day. This includes recognizing that you will be in your costume that whole time if you can't take it off. In our first competition, the woman who won wore full armor, but had to stand all day because there was no way to sit in it!

Conclusion: Find Yourself in Cosplay

We hope you will try cosplay, and we hope this book will help you.

This activity is fun, it's true, but it is also a great way to explore different ideas, different looks, and different ways of thinking about yourself.

In cosplay, you can be mean or sweet or intense or crazy for a day. You can be a girl or a boy or a robot or a monster for a while and see how that feels.

You'll meet others on the same journey of "playing" with their identities, and you will make life-long friends.

Come join the cosplay community- look us up online at www.cosplaymom.com or checkout Kiogenic on Twitter, Instagram, Tumblr or YouTube. Come find yourself with us. We'd love to include you!

About the Authors:

Cosplaymom is also known as Dr. Elizabeth Gackstetter Nichols. She's a professor of Spanish and Cultural Studies at Drury University in Springfield, Missouri. In her work life she specializes in beauty, beauty work and cosplay in Latin America and the United States. She has written many articles and books on beauty, including *Beauty, Virtue, Power and Success in Venezuela: 1850-2015.* She has two forthcoming articles on cosplay: "Weirdo Barbie and Country Punk Rocker: Gender, Identity and Appearance of Eleven in Stranger Things" and "Playing' with Identity: Storytelling, Performance and Feminine Agency in Cosplay." None of what she does would be possible without the amazing cosplay community.

Elizabeth is the lucky Mom of Kiogenic, an amazing cosplayer, artist and human, blessed wife of Tech Support, who always is willing to support the cosplay habit, and human to two cats, who mostly just shed on the cosplay. She blogs at www.cosplaymom.com

Kiogenic, is also known as Kira Nichols. She is a student in college studying graphic design and art at Webster University. She has been an avid cosplayer since 2013 and plans to be doing so for many years to come. Her best known cosplays are Yang Xaio Long, 2-D, Hiro Hamada and Elizabeth Comstock. You can see her work on her Instagram @kiogenic. She is grateful for the support and skills learned from her family and, of course, the late night moral support of her two cats.

Made in the USA
Columbia, SC
24 November 2021

49733584R00035